N E W   Y O R K   C I T Y

A   P H O T O G R A P H I C   P O R T R A I T

PETER BENNETT

First published in the United States
of America by:

Twin Lights Publishers, Inc.
10 Hale Street
Rockport, Massachusetts 01966
Telephone: (978) 546-7398
http://www.twinlightspub.com

ISBN 1-885435-46-0

10 9 8 7 6 5 4

Images of Rockefeller Center used
with permission of RCPI Landmark
Properties, L.L.C.

Editorial by
Rebecca Dominguez
http://www.FreelanceWriters.us

Book design by
SYP Design & Production, Inc.
http://www.sypdesign.com

Printed in China

The shoreline was dark and foreboding when New York's first immigrants arrived from Holland in the early 1600's, after a treacherous, two-month ocean crossing. There were no beacons of light to greet them, no tugboats to guide them, no torch of liberty, no Ellis Island to record their names. They arrived in surprisingly small groups of a few families and individuals, all who shared dreams of a better life in the New World.

One settler's letter in 1624 praised the abundances of New Amsterdam (New York City), "The woods abound with acorns for feeding hogs, and with venison. There is considerable fish in the rivers; good tillage land; here is, especially, free coming and going, without fear of the naked natives of the country."

Records show that Manhattan was purchased in 1626 from the native American Indians, who welcomed the settlers but didn't quite understand the concept of land ownership. By 1628, as one account described, "there already resided on the Island of the Manhatens, two hundred and

seventy souls, men, women and children, under Governor (Peter) Minuit...living there in peace with the Natives."

Today, nearly 400 years later, Manhattan is the largest city in America, with 12 million people throughout the Metropolitan area. It continues to attract foreign immigrants and Americans from cities and towns all over the country who come to realize their dreams.

New York is a vibrant, challenging city filled with the fruits of man's loftiest talents and accomplishments. It is here where the "envelope" is pushed every day. It is a city of "the biggest and the best." The song lyrics of New York New York describe its universal appeal:

These little town blues,
are melting away
I'll make a brand new start of it—
in old New York
If I can make it there,
I'll make it anywhere
It's up to you—
New York, New York

Colonnade Row, East Village
428-434 Lafayette Street

Colonnade Row, in the East Village's Soho neighborhood, offers sightseers a nostalgic look at homes of New York's rich and famous in the early 1800's. Unlike the typical row house, these four Greek Revival mansions were fashioned after London's Regent's Park. Built in 1833 by millionaires John Jacob Astor and Cornelius Vanderbilt, they were the most luxurious speculative row houses at that time. Famous residents over the years included Vanderbilt, Washington Irving, William Makepeace Thackery, and Charles Dickens. Today the once-elegant mansions have been renovated into million-dollar condominiums. The street level houses restaurants and the Colonnade Theater.

Rooftop, East Village

Take the last flight up to the rooftop and inhale the night air under a blanket of starlit skies. Listen to the muted noise below of a unique community considered by many as the last, authentic bohemian neighborhood in the City. The East Village struts its eccentricity like a beacon promising safe haven to creative and progressive thinkers. During the 1950's, artists migrated across Broadway from the West Village (Greenwich Village) to this rougher neighborhood. By the 1960's, beatnik philosophers Jack Kerouac and Allen Ginsberg were famous residents. Today, the tradition of the coffeehouse continues to set the tempo with avant-garde music and poetry.

◄ **Antique Shop, East Village**

The East Village is famous for its small, cluttered antique shops that tempt the passerby with promises of irresistible "finds."

▲ **Café Orlin, East Village**

Sidewalk tables at Café Orlin give diners a great meal and an entertaining view of the colorful personalities and unique rhythm of the East Village.

St. Mark's Church-in-the-Bowery, East Village

Founded in 1779, St. Mark's Church-in-the-Bowery is an active Episcopal church celebrating 200 years of community service and out-reach in its colorful East Village neighborhood. Many New Yorkers regard this landmark church as the "heart" of the East Village because of its world-renowned commitment to Ministry through the Arts. It is home to numerous artistic and performance groups, including the nationally acclaimed Poetry Project, one of the premier forums for innovative poetry in the United States. "The Poetry Project burns like red hot coal in New York's snow." —Allen Ginsberg (1926–1997)

**The Brooklyn Bridge,
East River**

Rising over the East River, this
landmark bridge lights up the
night sky with its magnificent
necklace of twinkling lights.

**Statue of Liberty and
Lower Manhattan**

Designed by Frederic-Auguste-
Bartholdi and given to us by the
French in 1884 to celebrate
America's Centennial, its official
title is Liberty Enlightening the
World.

◄ **Manhattan Kayak Company, Chelsea Piers**

Kayakers enjoy their own personal sightseeing boats when they take classes and tours with the region's largest kayak tour operator. Tours cover over 150 nautical miles of local waters.

⋏ **Lower Manhattan Skyline**

By far the best way to enjoy New York's dramatic harbor setting is to hop aboard a sightseeing boat with your camera loaded.

Woolworth Building, 233 Broadway

Soaring above City Hall Plaza, this famous building is a spectacular example of early 20th-century skyscrapers with its wide base, tall shaft, and triangular cap. Five-and-dime tycoon, Frank Woolworth's personal wish was a Gothic-style skyscraper in the tradition of London's Parliament buildings, which helped earn its nickname, Cathedral of Commerce. High ceilings create a 56-story skyscraper that is as tall as modern 80-story buildings. The interior lobby and hallways embrace the Gothic style with vaulted, stained glass mosaic ceilings, and ornamentations that include three humorous gargoyles depicting key people in the building's construction—the engineer, a bank president, and the building's rental agent.

The Sphere
Bronze Sculpture from Ground Zero

This monumental bronze and steel sculpture by German artist Fritz Koenig graced the fountain of the World Trade Center Plaza, since 1971, a symbol of peace through international trade. After the September 11th terrorist attacks, the 25-foot sphere is miraculously the only surviving piece of art from Ground Zero. Now the famous sculpture has a new home in Battery Park. *"The sphere that rests behind me in many ways symbolizes New York,"* New York Mayor Michael Bloomberg said in a ceremony six months after the attacks. *"On September 11th, it was damaged, not destroyed."*

◄ Old Ship, Battery Park

An historic ship is at anchor at Battery Park, a community at the tip of Manhattan on the Hudson River that is rich in colorful maritime history.

▲ South Street Seaport

A renovated American landmark in lower Manhattan, it houses the South Street Seaport Museum, home to the nation's largest in-water fleet of privately maintained historic vessels. The 1908 lightship Ambrose once guided ships safely from the ocean into New York Bay.

◄ Ellis Island Immigration Museum

The fourth largest museum in the City, it receives almost two million visitors annually—twice as many as entered here in 1907, Ellis Island's peak immigration year.

⋏ Ellis Island Immigration Museum , Grand Hall

Restoration of Ellis Island's 19th-century Beaux-Arts Main Building that houses the museum was completed in 1990, after eight years of meticulous craftsmanship.

Ellis Island

Over 100 million Americans today can trace their heritage in the United States to the 12 million immigrants who packed up their belongings, boarded a steamship, and landed at the Ellis Island depot between 1892 and 1954. Today their stories are chronicled in the award-winning Ellis Island Immigration Museum. Thirty galleries and multimedia exhibits trace our ancestors, footsteps into the actual rooms where they slept and the examination rooms where they were screened for diseases and disabilities. Continue up the "Stairway of Separation" to the great, echoing Registry Room, where a busy official decided each immigrant's fate.

◄ **Lower Manhattan Slyline from Ellis Island**

The short ferry ride to Ellis Island and the near-by Statue of Liberty rewards sightseers with breathtaking views of Lower Manhattan.

▲ **Winter Garden, World Financial Center**

This grand public space is the centerpiece of the World Financial Center.

➤ **Statue of Liberty**

This famous lady's island home sits atop Fort Wood, a Revolutionary War fortress shaped as an 11-point star. The statue was fully restored for its 100th birthday celebration in 1986.

◄ **Sidewalk Clock**

One block from Ground Zero on the corner of Broadway and Wall, this famous sidewalk clock outside of Barthman's Jewelry store is running right on time.

▲ **Wall Street Bull**

This massive bronze statue has long been Wall Street's mascot. Legend says that if you rub its nose, it will bring you good fortune.

New York Stock Exchange

The New York Stock Exchange (NYSE), at the corner of Broad and Wall Streets, is the heart beat of the financial district. One of the largest stock exchanges in the world, it is home to some 2,800 companies valued at nearly $15 trillion. The NYSE originated in 1792 when 24 stockbrokers signed a simple, two-sentence agreement. A year later, the group dedicated the Tontine Coffee House on Wall Street as the site of their exchange.

◄ Federal Hall, Wall Street

Federal Hall is rich in revolutionary history. The first U.S. Congress met here and wrote the Bill of Rights, and George Washington was inaugurated here in 1789.

⟁ Fraunces Tavern, Broad Street

Much of the Revolutionary history of New York revolved around Fraunces Tavern. When the war was won, Washington and his officers held a victory banquet here.

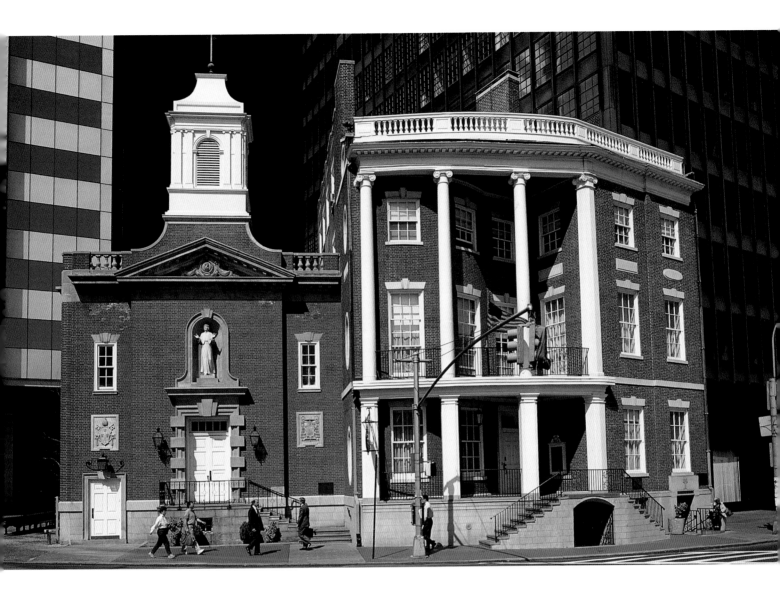

James Watson House, South Ferry

The Watson residence is the only survivor of the elegant Federal-style row houses that lined State Street and lower Broadway in the late eighteenth and early nineteenth centuries. These were the homes of prosperous sea captains and merchants who enjoyed unobstructed views of New York harbor and beyond to the hills of Staten Island, New Jersey, and Brooklyn. Today the Watson house is occupied by the Rectory of the Church of Our Lady of the Rosary.

◄ South Street Seaport

A thriving community on New York's historic waterfront, it is home to a world-class maritime museum, breathtaking views and hundreds of fashionable shops and restaurants.

⋏ Brooklyn Bridge

It is often said that inventions are made by impatient people. In 1855, John Roebling, a famous bridge designer, was impatient with the slow pace of the ferry as it crossed the East River. He designed and built a wonderful solution—the Brooklyn Bridge.

World Financial Center

As the sun goes down, workers in the World Financial Center cast an afternoon shadow on the plaza as they head home.

Battery Park

Battery Park sits at the tip of Manhattan, just below the financial district and was once a strategic artillery defense position for the English and Dutch. It is home to Castle Clinton, the city's only fort built right before the War of 1812. At one end of the 21-acre park is Hope Garden, a memorial for AIDS victims. At the other end, ferries depart regularly for the Statue of Liberty and Ellis Island. Street vendors like the one pictured here make sure that tourists don't go home empty handed.

**East Coast Memorial,
Battery Park**

Dedicated in 1963, this memorial dom-
inates the landscape of Battery Park
with eight 19-ft granite walls inscribed
with the name, rank, and home state
of 4,601 servicemen who lost their
lives in the Atlantic Ocean during
World War II. An imposing, art deco
eagle stands guard at the head of the
monument.

▲ Hudson River Park

This five-mile park meanders along the river front from Battery Park to 59th Street with never-ending views of boats, people, and the changing skyline.

**➤ Group of Four Trees
Chase Plaza**

Towering over the plaza is world-renowned artist Jean Dubuffet's 43-foot sculpture, Group of Four Trees. This alternative reality art-work has entertained people in the plaza since 1972.

Brooklyn Bridge, Pedestrian Walkway

"If there is to be a bridge," wrote one man in the 1800's, *"it must take one grand flying leap from shore to shore over the masts of the ships. There can be no piers or drawbridge ...only one great arch all the way across. Surely this must be a wonderful bridge."*

Today the recently refurbished Brooklyn Bridge, once the longest suspension bridge in the world, is a National Historic Landmark. Its pedestrian footbridge, as viewed from the Brooklyn side, is a popular walk for thousands of natives and tourists.

Manhattan Bridge

The last of the three great suspension bridges spanning the East River, the Manhattan Bridge opened to traffic in 1909. Today, nearly 100 years later, it is one of the most heavily traveled East River crossings, moving a daily average of 350,000 commuters and 78,000 vehicles between Canal Street in lower Manhattan and Brooklyn.

◄ **Lower Manhattan Skyline**

Dusk casts an orange hue of dramatic contrast against the dark silhouettes of Manhattan's downtown skyscrapers.

▲ **Aerial View, Lower Manhattan**

The twinkling lights of Lower Manhattan seem to go on forever with the Hudson River and New Jersey off to the distant right.

➤ **Statue of Liberty**

When Lady Liberty came into view from ships steaming into the Harbor, the sight brought tears of joy to millions of immigrants who knew that they were finally free and safe.

◄ **Staten Island Ferry**

One guide book calls it "One of the world's greatest (and shortest) water voyages." Every day 70,000 passengers hop aboard for their daily 25-minute commute into Manhattan.

⋏ **Brooklyn and Manhattan Bridges**

These suspension bridges over the East River are just two of many engineering triumphs that helped unite the five boroughs of New York.

World Financial Center

The four office towers of the World Financial Center in Battery Park City house the world headquarters of prestigious international corporations such as American Express and Merrill Lynch. Public spaces connect the four office towers and include the glass-enclosed Winter Garden (*page 18*), and the outdoor Plaza, a European-styled Courtyard. The Center is also home to an innovative and popular series of performing and visual arts programs that are presented in the public spaces of the complex.

Broadway Ticker Tape Parade

Many of the world's greatest triumphs have been celebrated with spectacular ticker-tape parades up Broadway. From atop their convertibles, politicians, war veterans, sports stars and astronauts have all been dazzled by the surrealism of roaring crowds and the blizzard of ticker tape. Broadway has long been known as the Canyon of Heroes and will soon commemorate each of the 200 ticker-tape parades with its own black granite strip in the sidewalk, beginning with the historic first parade in 1886 celebrating the Statue of Liberty.

City Hall, Yankees World Champions, 1999

The streets were packed with Yankee enthusiasts, but the best seats in the city were the invitation-only seats at City Hall. Hundreds of colorful balloons were released into clear, blue skies as politicians, dignitaries, and celebrities applauded.

◄ **Greenwich Village, Grove Court**

Greenwich Village is an alley-hunter's dream, with plenty of "mapped" alleys as well as private ones, like Grove Court, that keep the public out with locked, gated walls. Interestingly, Grove Court was originally built around 1850 for laborers and tradesmen.

⋀ **Greenwich Village, Bank Street**

Bank Street is one of those delightful, tree-lined streets in the Village with quaint, Federal-style town houses and ivy-covered brownstones.

LET US RAISE A STANDARD TO WHICH THE WISE
AND THE HONEST CAN REPAIR   THE EVENT
IS IN THE HAND OF GOD   ★   WASHINGTON

Washington Square Park

You can sit for hours in this historic park in the heart of Greenwich Village, watching the colorful parade of students, performance artists, skateboarders, chess players and dog lovers. This 10-acre city park is well known for its bohemian setting and passionate community activities, and is characterized by the large, central fountain and triumphal stone arch. The arch was conceived as part of the 1889 centennial celebrations of George Washington's Presidential inauguration on the steps of Federal Hall.

Cafe Wha? Greenwich Village

"You'd be hard pressed to find a more exhilarating evening out than Café Wha?" raved an entertainment critic at the New York Post, summing up this unique Greenwich Village club. It's one of the nightspots where Bob Dylan, Jimi Hendrix and other 60's legendary musicians polished their styles and launched their careers. Tuesday is the club's famous funk night which always attracts a big crowd and celebrities.

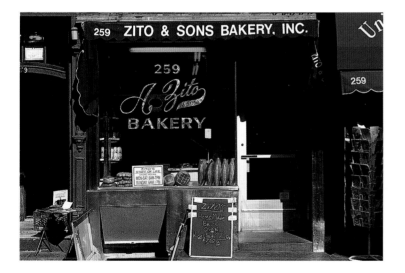

◄ **Zito's Bakery, Greenwich Village**

The aroma of fresh baked bread filling the air on Bleecker Street comes from one of the oldest and most famous bakeries in the Village. Baking is done in cast-iron stoves that date back to the American Civil War.

▲ **Village Cigars, Greenwich Village**

Located at the corner of Sheridan Square and Christopher Street, this famous retailer of fine, handmade cigars is known for its great selection and prices.

◄ **Bleeker Street,
Greenwich Village**

In 19th-century New York,
Bleecker Street was known as
the French Quarter which
explains the special charm today
of its quaint specialty shops and
sidewalk cafés.

⋏ **Charles Street,
Greenwich Village**

When you take a stroll down
Charles Street, with its elegant
brownstones and beautiful land-
scaping, it's easy to imagine a
quieter time in 19th-century
New York.

➤ **Leroy Street,
Greenwich Village**

When these 19th-century
brownstones were built,
Greenwich Village was a quiet
residential neighborhood far
from the hustle and bustle of
the city's business district to
the south.

◄ **Flatiron Building, 5th Ave. and Broadway**

This famous landmark building's most interesting feature is its shape. A mere six feet wide at its apex, it expands into a limestone wedge adorned with Gothic and Renaissance details of Greek faces and terra cotta flowers.

⋀ **Midtown Manhattan**

Skyscrapers sparkle in the golden hues of a setting sun in Midtown, home to the largest concentration of skyscrapers in the city.

Post Office, Main Branch

Built in 1913, this imposing building with its Corinthian-columned edifice bears the famous words: Neither snow, nor rain, nor heat, nor gloom of night shall stay these couriers from the swift completion of their appointed rounds.

◄ 5th Avenue Building Clock

This beautiful 1909 gold street clock in front of the Fifth Avenue Building is framed by the landmark Flatiron Building and the American flag.

▲ Grand Central Terminal

After a $179-million-dollar restoration, this splendid station is becoming a hive of retail and cultural activity while it continues to transport millions of regional commuters.

➤ Grand Central Terminal

Mercury, the Greek god of merchants, presides over the stunning Beaux Arts architecture of the largest railroad terminal in the world.

GRAND CENTRAL
TERMINAL

◄ **Midtown Manhattan**

In the nighttime landscape, the streetlights and traffic seem to flow right to the Empire State Building.

▲ **Midtown Manhattan from Hudson River**

Under a full moon, the Empire State Building twinkles high above a city of skyscrapers.

Empire State and Chrysler Buildings

The Empire State Building was the winner of a spirited "Race to the Sky" competition between automotive tycoons Walter Chrysler of the Chrysler Corporation and John Raskob of General Motors to see who could build the highest building first. Completed ahead of schedule and under budget in 1931, the 102-story Empire State Building was the tallest building in the world for 40 years until the World Trade Center rose higher.

◄ **Empire State Building**

The communications tower atop this famous landmark was originally designed to be an anchor for dirigibles, a popular mode of air travel in the 1930's.

⋏ **Penn Plaza and Madison Square Garden**

Home of the Knicks and the Rangers, the Garden also produces major theatrical events and hosts corporate business events.

◄ **Midtown from Hudson River**

Framed by the Chrysler Building (*far left*) and the Empire State Building (*far right*) this midtown slice of Manhattan skyscrapers rises majestically above the Hudson River.

⋀ **Met Life and Chrysler Buildings**

The setting sun lights up the modern MetLife Building and the art deco details of the Chrysler building's steeple.

Penn Plaza

Adjacent to Madison Square Garden, this 57-story office tower rises from a complex of low-rise shops and restaurants. It covers an entire city block in midtown Manhattan, and has direct access to nearby Pennsylvania Station. The original Penn Station was a grandiose 19th-century railroad terminal in the Beaux Arts style of Grand Central Station, but fell to the wrecking ball to build the new Madison Square Garden. The trains still run below ground level.

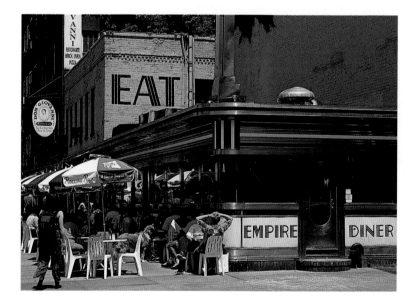

◄ Empire Diner, Chelsea

The "Open" sign is always lit at this famous Chelsea diner, built in 1946 to resemble a railroad dining car. Today it still delivers good, reasonable food in an authentic diner atmosphere.

⋀ Old Stable, Chelsea

This old stable in the historic Chelsea neighborhood is a quaint reminder of the era of horse-drawn carriages and cobblestone streets.

Ornate Door, Chelsea

A once, downtrodden neighborhood, Chelsea is now one of the premier areas of Manhattan's westside and features quiet streets lined with ornate 19th century row houses.

⊼ Empire State Building

It's not hard for the most famous skyscraper in the world to loom over its diminutive neighboring buildings in midtown Manhattan.

➤ Patriotic Colors

Resplendent in patriotic colors, the Empire State Building wears different colors and designs to celebrate national holidays.

New York Skyline from Hudson River

Midtown Manhattan shines across the Hudson River in this perfect panoramic slice. Even in the early 19th century, the city's influential visionaries were setting the stage with their ambitious plans for transforming this colonial town into the most powerful city in the world.

Over time, the city grew in leaps and bounds, claiming more space from the southern tip of Manhattan to the north. Great bridges reached across the surrounding waters and created vital connections to Brooklyn and Queens on Long Island, The Bronx, Staten Island, and northern New

Jersey. Tunnels burrowed under the Hudson and East Rivers to accommodate more traffic. Thanks to the indomitable spirit of those visionaries, New York City is like no other city in the world. Its center is filled with the lush beauty of Central Park, the largest public park in the country, surrounded

by thousands of architectural wonders from the 19th and 20th centuries.

Best of all, the city is home to a colorful tapestry of people from all over the world who energize the city with unparalleled ethnic and cultural diversity.

◄ Green Street, Soho

You never know what you'll find wandering around these cobblestoned streets. Antiques, chic boutiques, art galleries, restaurants and bars beckon with their charms.

▲ Prince Street and West Broadway, Soho

Soho is a visual feast and one of the best areas in New York to shop, eat, and just walk around.

Cast Iron Building, Soho

The unique flavor of Soho derives from being home to the greatest collection of historic, landmark cast-iron buildings in the world. Popular in the mid-1800's, cast-iron molds faithfully duplicated the most intricate architectural details and gave buildings an inexpensive face-lift. At the turn of the century, as fashionable businesses moved uptown, Soho became a slum of sweatshops known as "Hell's Hundred Acres." By the 1960's, artists began to move into the abandoned, "lofty" spaces. The rebirth of Soho began.

◄ Midtown New York

Midtown Manhattan spreads out in a blanket of twinkling lights with the green-jeweled necklace of the Brooklyn Bridge on the far horizon to the left.

▲ Felix Restaurant, Soho

This popular Parisian-style bistro on West Broadway is just one of a delicious variety of eateries in Soho.

Spring Street, Soho

An acronym for SOuth of HOuston Street, Soho is an eclectic neighborhood in lower Manhattan that has traveled a long, hard way to become the City's artistic haven. In the 60's and 70's, starving artists moved into the spacious and cheap warehouse spaces. Today's Soho is quite different. Renovated loft apartments now sell in the millions and the fantastic boutiques, galleries, and restaurants that line the cobblestone streets appeal to a more well-heeled clientele.

▲ 6th Avenue Buildings

A clever camera angle transforms 6th Avenue skyscrapers into an imposing phalanx of giants.

➤ Rockefeller Center

The Greek god Prometheus, shimmering in gold, lords over the plaza at Rockefeller Center in midtown. Prometheus is the legendary protector and benefactor of man.

Atlas Statue, Rockefeller Center

When plans for Rockefeller Center were unveiled in 1930, people couldn't comprehend its scope. Today, far bigger than the original center, it is an intimate urban space comprised of 23 buildings with the towering 70-story GE Building at its center.

Rockefeller Center

Rockefeller Center's public spaces are as impressive as the buildings themselves. The Plaza is a multi-leveled pedestrian space surrounding a skating rink in winter and an outdoor café in summer.

◄ **New York Public Library**

"The lions without, the learning within"

A pair of lions greet holiday visitors ascending the massive front steps of the Main Library. When completed in 1911, this landmark Beaux Arts building was the largest marble structure in the United States.

▲ **Macy's, Herald Square, 34th Street**

Macy's Herald Square, the world's largest store, thrills shoppers with over 400,000 different items including fashions for the family and furnishings for the home.

**New York Public Library,
5th Avenue and 42nd Street**

As the 19th century drew to a close,
the greatest city in America still had no
real public library. But thanks to a
handful of visionaries and millions of
users, the library today is internation-
ally recognized as one of the greatest
institutions of its kind. Computer tech-
nology now makes its vast resources
available to users worldwide. Number-
ing into the tens of millions, its hold-
ings proudly include the Gutenberg
Bible and Jefferson's manuscript copy
of the Declaration of Independence.

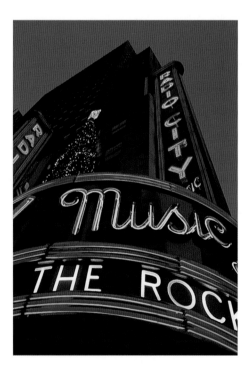

◄ Radio City Music Hall

A central part of the Radio City Music Hall experience is The Rockettes, its famous line of high-kicking dancers.

▲ Prudential Financial Building

The Prudential Financial Building rounds the corner at 42nd Street and 7th Avenue in the heart of the Theater District.

➤ Radio City Music Hall

The sumptuous 5,874-seat Radio City Music Hall (1932) is an Art Deco delight, designed as a palatial entertainment center affordable to the general public.

◄ Streets of Times Square

This famous intersection in the middle of the Theater District conjures up the colorful sights and sounds of live theater that has entertained audiences for decades.

▲ Times Square

The bright lights of Time Square beckon aspiring actors, singers and dancers as well as theater goers who love the special thrill of live theater.

Ford Center for the Performing Arts

This lavish theater is constructed on the site of two classic houses, the Lyric and the Apollo and incorporates original architectural elements from both theaters. State-of-the-art facilities make it possible to produce grand-scale musicals like the long-running hit 42nd Street.

◄ **Rockefeller Center**

Millions of people have come to the annual Christmas Tree Lighting ceremony at Rockefeller Center since the tradition began in 1933.

⋀ **The Late Show with David Letterman**

Letterman's record-breaking nightly show in the GE building at Rockefeller Plaza has enjoyed a successful run for over 10 years.

➤ **Christmas, 6th Avenue**

When Christmas comes to 6th Avenue, one building's holiday spirit seems to outdo the next, and every passerby reaps the rewards.

tkts

The line can get quite long at this famous ticket window on the center island of Duffy Square in the Theater District. But it's well worth the wait. TKTS sells unsold tickets on the day of performance for all Broadway shows at a friendly 25–50% discount off the box-office price. Established in 1973 for the betterment of theaters and theater-goers, TKTS is doing a wonderful job of filling seats and making the theater experience accessible to a wider variety of people.

Algonquin Hotel

Historic Traveler magazine calls it *"One of America's 10 Best Historic Hotels."* The Algonquin certainly earns its reputation for charm and ambiance. This elegant hotel has always attracted the rich and famous, but none became more famous than a group of aspiring, young journalists and columnists know as the Algonquin Round Table who met there regularly for 10 years. Known for their rapier wit, founding members such as drama critics Dorothy Parker and Aleck Woolcott and columnist Heywood Braun lived by the motto, *"Eat, drink and be merry for tomorrow we all shall die."*

◄ **P. J. Clarke's Bar, 3rd Avenue**

P.J. Clarke's is a legendary neighborhood bar and restaurant in business since the 1860's. The lavish 19th century decor features stained glass domes, rich mahogany trim, and mosaic tiles.

▲ **The Waldorf Astoria, Park Avenue**

This world famous Art Deco hotel takes up an entire city block. It has always been a home away from home to heads of state and every US president since Hoover.

Park Avenue

Driving down Park Avenue with its broad center island, you can easily see why it has always been a popular place where New York's wealthy and fashionable live, shop, and dine. In the distance, the formidable MetLife Building redirects avenue traffic around its massive base.

◄ Grand Central Station

In this historic railroad station, a clock gives commuters the most important information they need: will they be on time to catch their regular train home?

⋀ Madison Avenue

The traffic never stops on this business avenue. In the daytime, it offers some of the best shopping in the world.

St. Bartholomew's Church, Park Avenue and 50th Street

"St. Bart's," with its dramatic Romanesque architecture, is one of New York City's great landmark churches with a rich tradition of community outreach. In the late 19th century, the ministry helped the waves of new immigrants who were living in slums. Today the church continues its outreach with a homeless shelter, soup kitchen, and food bank.

Chrysler Building

The 77-story Chrysler Building is one of New York's magnificent monuments of the Art Deco style that was introduced in Paris in 1925. The building's cloud-piercing spire and gleaming, steel-clad ornament, depicting gargoyles, hub-caps, and the winged helmets of Mercury, symbolized the excitement of the Machine Age. It was the tallest building in the world at the time it was finished, but the Empire State Building grabbed that title just one year later.

United Nations

The United Nation's world headquarters, adjacent to the East River, is a familiar sight in the New York skyline. At the close of World War II in 1945, the UN was created by 51 countries who were committed to serving peace through international cooperation and collective security. Today 91 countries are members, representing nearly every country in the world. It is a popular attraction for tourists, natives, and school groups.

◄ Shakespeare Garden, Central Park

This serene cottage rock garden replicates the plants and flowers of Shakespeare's English garden. A perfect retreat for a peaceful park experience.

▲ Stone Bridge, Central Park

One of the urban wonders of the world, Central Park is such a natural part of the Manhattan environment that many people don't realize it is entirely man-made.

► Belvedere Castle, Central Park

Built as a fantasy structure by park designer Frederick Law Olmstead, the castle is on a high rock formation and rewards visitors with panoramic views.

Reservoir, Central Park

The Reservoir is known for its spectacular views of the city as well as for the
1.58-mile running track that encircles
it. At one time, the city's water supply
came from here, but now the reservoir
supplies water for Park facilities. The
106-acre body of water attracts a colorful variety of wildlife. Bird-watchers
have spotted five species of gulls and
over 20 species of waterfowl, grebes,
cormorants, and loons.

◄ **Carousel, Central Park**

This elegant carousel was once powered by a mule and a real horse. Today adults and children can't resist the thrill of riding the biggest, hand-carved jumping horses in the world.

⋏ **Bethesda Fountain, Central Park**

Beautiful landscapes and water-scapes, formal walkways, and the magnificent fountain sculpture, Angel of the Waters, all converge at the popular Bethesda Terrace.

◄ **Cyclists, Central Park**

Central Park is a cyclist's heaven. The park's 6.03-mile circular path is the most popular bicycling route in Manhattan.

⋀ **The Lake, Central Park**

Lake visitors in a more romantic mood can rent a gondola, just like the authentic Venetian craft that crossed the Lake in the 19th century.

Sheep Meadow, Central Park

Central Park was the first landscaped park in the United States designed completely for public use. As true 19th-century romantics, park designers Frederick Law Olmstead and Calvert Vaux also trusted in the power of nature to lift man's spirit above the drudgery of city life. They created an 843-acre pastoral landscape in the English romantic tradition with open rolling meadows like Sheep Meadow (home to a shepherd and his flock of sheep for many years), wild gardens, wilderness forest trails and the formal public spaces, The Mall and Bethesda Terrace.

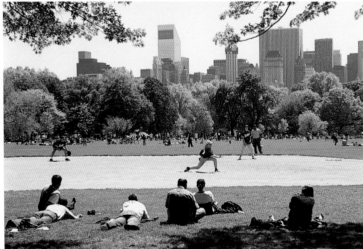

◅ **The Great Lawn, Central Park**

On warm summer nights, New Yorkers head for the Great Lawn, the largest open space in the Park, for free performances of the Philharmonic or the Metropolitan Opera.

⋀ **The Mall, Central Park**

The Mall is the central promenade into the heart of Central Park, filled with the excitement of skaters, dancers, musicians and delighted spectators.

The Lake, Central Park

Created out of a large swamp, the 22-acre lake originally was designed for boating in the summer and ice-skating in the winter. When the Wollman Ice Skating Rink opened in 1950, the lake returned to its natural habitat. Today the lake is a quiet retreat where boaters and landlubbers enjoy the lake vistas and the graceful swans and ducks.

▲ **Alma Mater, Columbia University, "Nurturing Mother"**

The Alma Mater bronze statue in front of the University's Law Library, is the inspiration for the nickname people call their university or college.

➤ **Riverside Church, Riverside Drive**

This magnificent interdenominational church, modeled after the famous 13th-century gothic cathedral in Chartres, France, seats over 2,000 worshipers.

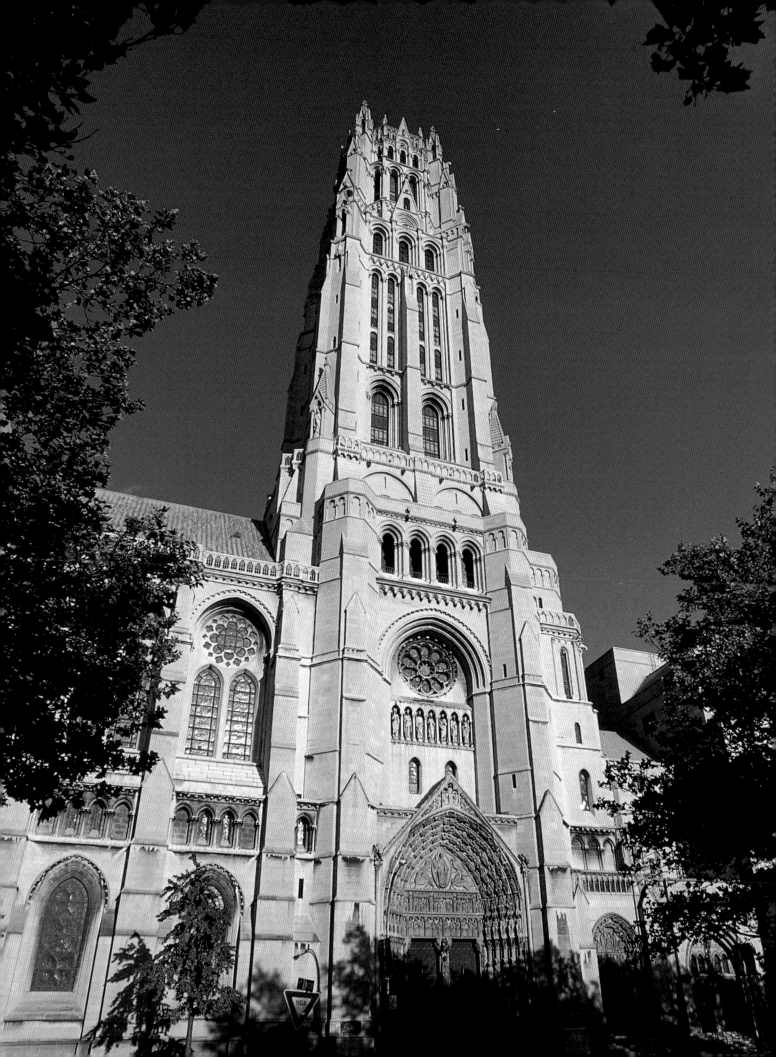

◄ George Washington Bridge

The George Washington Bridge crosses a curve in the Hudson River and connects upper Manhattan to the commuter suburbs of Northern New Jersey.

▲ Riverside Park

Stretching for several miles on Manhattan's Upper West Side, this waterfront parkland rewards visitors with spectacular views of the Hudson River and the George Washington Bridge.

Trump International Hotel

This luxurious steel and glass building soars above the southwestern gateway of Central Park at Columbus Circle and is convenient to the finest shops and restaurants of Madison and Fifth avenues. Telescopes are provided for spectacular New York skyline gazing.

Museum of Natural History

Museum visitors usually remember the first time they stood next to the dinosaurs. We all enjoy watching the animated dinosaurs in movies like Jurassic Park; it's quite another experience to stand next to the real thing and realize that even the skeleton is quite scarey!

Lincoln Center for the Performing Arts

There is always something marvelous and exciting going on at Lincoln Center, the world's largest cultural complex. It is home to 12 world-renowned independent companies that represent the very best in the performing arts today. Visitors can tour the Metropolitan Opera House, Avery Fisher Hall, and New York State Theater. Resident companies include The New York City Ballet, The New York Philharmonic, The Julliard School and the School of American Ballet, to name a few.

◄ Rose Center for Earth and Space, Museum of Natural History

A spiral walkway winds down from the new planetarium to the gallery's floor amidst scale models of stars, galaxies and planets suspended from the ceiling.

⋀ Museum of Natural History

A statue of President Theodore Roosevelt greets visitors to one of the most famous tourist attractions in the City, renowned for its millions of artifacts of the earth's evolution.

Rose Center for Earth and Space, Museum of Natural History

The new Rose Center, which replaced the old Hayden Planetarium, looks like it came straight out of a science fiction story. It is a clear glass cube, which is dominated by the sphere of the new planetarium theater. The Rose Center also displays provocative exhibits including a history of the Universe from the Big Bang until now, models of various stellar bodies, and an ecosystem contained inside a glass ball.

Isabella's, Columbus Avenue

Diners at this Upper West Side restaurant enjoy delicious food and a great view of the special rhythm of this trendy neighborhood.

Restaurant Row, Clinton

Formerly known as Hell's Kitchen, this area of Manhattan is fast becoming a desirable location on the west side due to its central location, its views of the Hudson River and mid-town skyscrapers, and a mouth-watering variety of eateries like this stretch of 46th Street called Restaurant Row.

◣ Claremont Riding Academy

Claremont is the oldest continu-
ously operated stable in the
United States. Today it is a riding
school and a place to rent a
horse to explore the six miles of
bridle paths in Central Park.

➤ 5th Avenue

Popular in song lyrics and movie
settings, 5th Avenue is where
New York's wealthy live in elegant apartments and spacious
penthouses with fantastic
Central Park views.

Guggenheim Museum

Frank Lloyd Wright ignored the conventional approach to museum design of interconnected, rectangular rooms. Instead, visitors are whisked to the top of the building by elevator. They view the art by descending at a leisurely pace on the gentle slope of a continuous ramp. The open rotunda gives visitors simultaneous views of several bays of work on different levels. The spiral design recalls a nautilus shell, with continuous spaces flowing freely one into another.

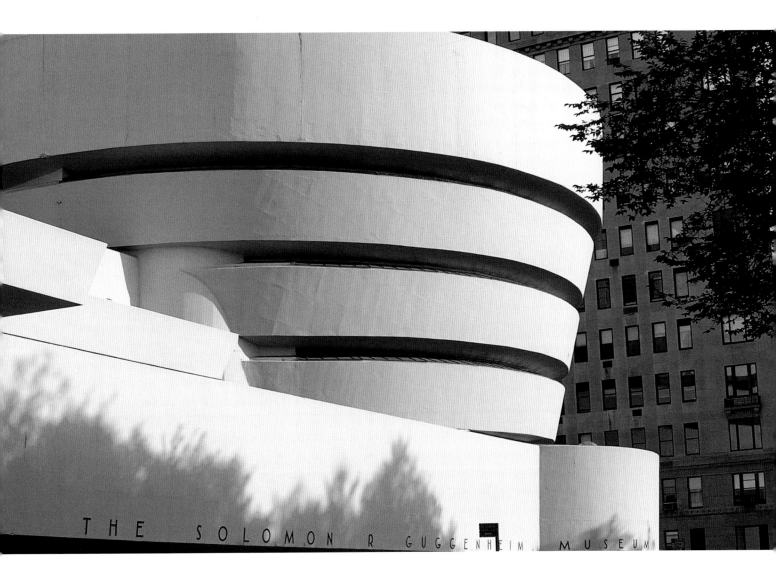

Guggenheim Museum

The architecture of this museum is as famous as the modern art that it houses. Frank Lloyd Wright conceived of its curving, continuous space as a temple of the spirit where viewers could foster a new way of looking at art. The museum's benefactor, Solomon R. Guggenheim, built it to house the radical new forms of art being developed by such artists as Vasily Kandinsky, Paul Klee, and Piet Mondrian. Today the museum excites visitors as much as it did the day it opened in 1959.

Elaine's, East Side Manhattan

Elaine's is a great place to star-watch New York's film literati and intellectual elite who come to savor Elaine's Italian-Jewish comfort food. Woody Allen dines here at least once a week. Despite the A-list crowd, Elaine's is a homey, no-frills kind of place, with red-painted walls and talk radio buzzing in the background.

5th Avenue

Christmas is a time for the upscale stores on Fifth Avenue to light up the street with colorful decorations. Even when motorists are frustrated with traffic jams, they can still enjoy the spectacle.

◄ **European Paintings, Metropolitan Museum of Art**

One of the world's greatest collections of Old Master and 19th-century European paintings, it features 2,200 works, including dozens of world-renowned artists.

⋀ **Temple of Dendur, Metropolitan Museum of Art**

The centerpiece of the museum's world-renowned Egyptian collection is the Temple of Dendur, an entire Roman-period temple (circa 15 BC) donated by the Egyptian government.

American Wing, Metropolitan Museum of Art

The American Wing of the largest art
museum in the Western Hemisphere
features one of the Museum's loveliest
and most popular spaces. The Charles
Engelhard Court is a spacious glassed-
in garden filled with large-scale
American sculptures, leaded-glass win-
dows, and other distinctive architectural elements. Since 1870, the Museum's
world-class collections have grown to
more than two million works of art
from all over the world, from ancient
through modern times.

◄ Hamilton Grange National Memorial, Harlem

This landmark district is rich in Revolutionary War history. George Washington's headquarters were here briefly in 1776 and his troops engaged in several skirmishes with the British troops.

▲ Hamilton Terrace, Harlem

This national historic district in Harlem is named after Alexander Hamilton, the nation's first Secretary of the Treasury, who lived here in the early 1800's.

➤ Grant's Tomb, Upper West Side

This memorial to General Ulysses S. Grant, victorious Union commander of the Civil War, includes the tomb shared by the General and his wife.

Times Square Subway Station

Pay $2.00 and you can travel on one of the most efficient people transportation systems in the world. No longer hot and dingy, the New York City Subway System has been completely renovated into a safe and comfortable mode of transportation between most areas of New York City.

Taxi in Manhattan

Natives and tourists agree that taking a New York taxi is an adventure in itself—if you can hail one in the first place—and can be more exciting than an amusement park ride! Good or bad, taxis are a critical mode of transportation that carries over 250,000 passengers daily.

4th of July Fireworks

Every year Macy's world-famous
4th of July fireworks continue to
dazzle and awe the crowds with
orchestrated explosions from
barges in the river. Spectators
will tell you that just when you
think the fireworks can't get any
better, they do!

The Brooklyn Bridge

The most famous 4th of July fireworks display in the country is caught in a perfect moment from the vantage point of the magnificent Brooklyn Bridge. The bridge itself earned its own fireworks show, parade, and flotilla of tall ships when New Yorkers celebrated its 100th anniversary in 1983.

The Williamsburg Bridge

Completed in 1903, the Williamsburg
Bridge became the world's longest suspension bridge for the next 20 years,
taking over the position previously held
by the Brooklyn Bridge. It is the largest
of the three suspension bridges that
span the East River. The bridge's
designer, Leffert L. Buck, was said to
have been inspired by the architect of
the Eiffel Tower.

The George Washington Bridge

"When your car moves up the ramp,
the two towers rise so high that it
brings you happiness; their structure is
so pure, so resolute, so regular that
here, finally, steel architecture seems
to laugh…"
—Swiss Architect Le Crobusier

Chinatown, Lower Manhattan

Walk down the narrow, crowded streets of Chinatown and you'll soon feel like you actually are in China. This community has the largest population of Chinese immigrants in the Western Hemisphere. This vibrant area is teeming with the aromas of hundreds of ethnic restaurants. Stores spill their goods onto the sidewalk to stop you in your tracks with live poultry in cages, whole fish, exotic fruits and vegetables, colorful Chinese housewares and souvenirs. It is a must-see tourist attraction, because the majority of Chinese New Yorkers actually live here.

Dragon Dance, Chinatown

Dragons are deeply rooted in Chinese culture and folklore. The Chinese consider themselves descendants of the dragon, a mythical symbol of prowess, nobility and fortune. The popularity of the dragon dance dates back to10th century China and is considered an indispensable part of most Asian festivals, especially the Chinese New Year.

◄ **Coney Island Arcade**

Coney Island was the birthplace of the first Amusement Park in 1895 and eventually became home to several of the largest amusement parks in the world.

▲ **Coney Island Beach**

"Heaven at the End of a Subway ride"

Coney Island Beach is the closest beach to Manhattan, so it's no wonder it soon became a favorite getaway from the noise and fast pace of the City.

Coney Island Rollercoaster

Since 1927, The Cyclone has been the number one attraction in Coney Island, and now it is also an official City landmark. The infamous Cyclone is a monumental twister that whistles along a wooden track, making steep rises and falls and tight twists and turns. The screams of happily terrified riders can be heard even before the top of the first rise is reached. It was built on the same historic site as the world's first roller coaster.

Willow Street, Brooklyn Heights

This East River community is Brooklyn's answer to Greenwich Village. Its tree-lined streets are home to elegant brownstones and stately apartment buildings. An 1850's city directory lists occupations of several residents as shipmaster, merchant, furrier, ice merchant, boarding house owner, writing master, lawyer, watchmaker, and grain measurer. Brooklyn Heights boasts of fantastic views of Manhattan and easy access to all parts of the City.

Bayridge Neighborhood, Brooklyn

After a yellow fever epidemic nearly wiped out the community of what was then known as Yellow Hook, a group of wealthy landowners gave the ravaged community a new name and a new beginning in 1853—Bayridge.

Today this thriving bayside community's reverence for its past and pride in its heritage are obvious with its many fine examples of historic 19th-century brownstones, mansions and churches.

**Enid A. Haupt Conservatory,
The New York Botanical Gardens,
The Bronx**

For nearly a century, the centerpiece
and symbol of The New York Botanical
Gardens has been its Conservatory,
one of the most beautiful Victorian-era
glass houses in the world. In 1997,
after a $25 million restoration, it now
houses A World of Plants, an unprece-
dented exhibition that gives visitors a
grand ecotour of the flora and fauna
of tropical, subtropical, and desert
environments.

Brooklyn Botanical Gardens

Growing from its humble beginnings as an ash dump in the late 1800's, the Brooklyn Botanical Garden today has come to represent the very best in urban gardening and horticultural displays. Visitors to this popular attraction always find something beautiful to see regardless of the season. In the 1950's, the BBG's research led to plant patents for weeping crabapples and yellow magnolias.

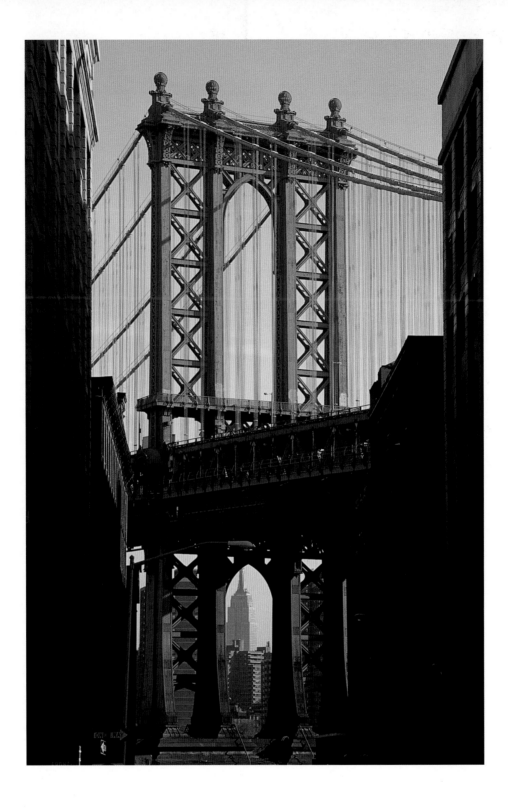

▲ **Manhattan Bridge**

From the great span of the Manhattan Bridge, the Empire State Building in mid-town is perfectly framed within a bridge support.

➤ **Unisphere, Flushing Meadow Park, Queens**

This giant steel model of the earth is a reminder of the World's Fair that took place in the Park in 1964–65. Today the park is home to the New York Mets and a world-class tennis center which hosts the U.S. Open, an annual Grand Slam event.

PETER BENNETT

Raised in Manhattan's Greenwich Village, Peter Bennett has been photographing New York City's streets, buildings and people for over twenty-five years. He is the owner of New York Stock Photo, an agency specializing in images of New York, and serves on the Board of Directors of Creative Eye/MIRA, an international photographers cooperative and stock agency. His work appears regularly in numerous publications, ads and calendars around the world and is also available as fine art prints. Prints of images in this book are available at www.ambientimages.com.